THE MEANING OF
PRESTIGE

CAMBRIDGE
UNIVERSITY PRESS

University Printing House, Cambridge CB2 8BS, United Kingdom

Published in the United States of America by Cambridge University Press, New York

Cambridge University Press is part of the University of Cambridge.

It furthers the University's mission by disseminating knowledge in the pursuit of education, learning and research at the highest international levels of excellence.

www.cambridge.org
Information on this title: www.cambridge.org/9781107650657

© Cambridge University Press 1937

First published 1937
First paperback edition 2014

A catalogue record for this publication is available from the British Library

ISBN 978-1-107-65065-7 Paperback

THE
MEANING OF PRESTIGE

by

HAROLD NICOLSON

THE REDE LECTURE
DELIVERED BEFORE THE UNIVERSITY
OF CAMBRIDGE ON
23 APRIL
1937

CAMBRIDGE
AT THE UNIVERSITY PRESS
1937

THE
MEANING OF PRESTIGE

It may seem curious that in accepting the honour of this ancient lectureship I should have chosen as my subject a theme which, at first sight, seems to bear as little relation to modern political theory as it does to the three branches of 'humanity, logic and philosophy' ordained by Sir Robert Rede in his endowment of 29 December 1518. I trust however that, as my argument proceeds, it will be agreed that the 'Meaning of Prestige' is in fact not un-related to that lack of clear political thinking which is the menace of our times; and in ex-amining the various interpretations which are, and have been, given to the word 'prestige' I shall endeavour to respect my terms of re-ference and to approach the problem in a frame of mind, both logical, philosophic and humane.

The title, and subject, of this lecture first occurred to me during a recent visit to Central Africa and the Sudan. How comes it, I asked myself, that we rule these dependencies with so modest an exhibition of the apparatus of power? How comes it that a mere handful of Englishmen—rare specks of foam upon a wide dark sea—can impose this habit of obedience upon so many millions? How comes it that, even after a resounding diplomatic defeat, our reputation does not durably decline? How comes it that after the most overt betrayals on our part we are still trusted and even revered? How comes it that our armament programme is nowhere—not even in Italy or Germany—regarded as a menace; and almost everywhere hailed with satisfaction and relief? And how comes it that what we carelessly call 'British prestige' is so different in quality from the various forms of national glory and honour which are worshipped and pursued elsewhere?

Such are the questions which I should wish to examine this morning.

I

The word 'prestige' derives from the Latin verb *praestringere* as generally employed in the phrase *praestringere oculos*, 'to bind or dazzle the eyes'. From this verb comes the even more disreputable substantive *praestigia*, which means nothing more nor less than 'jugglers' tricks'.

Our grandfathers, being more familiar with the humanities than we are to-day, were well aware of the low origins of the word 'prestige': αἰδώς, wrote Mr Gladstone in 1868, 'means honour, but never that base-born thing in these last times called prestige.' Freeman, in 1895, was even more explicit. 'Prestige', he wrote, 'I always like to have a pop at; I take it it has never lost its first meaning of conjuring tricks.' It must be admitted, however, that even in the 'sixties, even by a great scholar, the word could be employed with exactly that eulogistic connotation which we lend it to-day. 'Balliol', wrote Mark Pattison, 'can set off a prestige of long standing against a deficiency in the stipend.' Obviously, in such a context, there can be no possible suggestion of illusion, trickery or fraud.

The consideration remains, however, that it is only in the last fifty years that the word 'prestige' has acquired in English-speaking countries the honourable position which it to-day enjoys in our vocabulary and in that of the Dominions and the Colonies. For most Englishmen the word has lost all association with jugglers or conjurers, and has come to mean, as in the definition given by the Oxford English Dictionary: '*Influence or reputation derived from previous character, achievements or associations; or especially from past success.*'

I emphasise that definition since I shall use it as a thread upon which to string my argument. That argument will consist of three main questions and of the answers to those questions. My first question will be: 'Does the word prestige possess a universal meaning or does the meaning vary in different countries?' My answer to that question will be that, not only does the meaning of prestige vary in the several languages, but that the general concept also changes in accordance with the political philosophies of the several nations. My second question will be: 'Assuming therefore that the meaning of prestige is particular and not universal, what is the interpretation of the word which is particular to the British people?' My answer to that question will be that the particular meaning of prestige in our own philosophy is: 'Power based upon reputation rather than reputation based upon power.' And my third question will be: 'Is it possible to-day for power based upon reputation to maintain itself against reputation based on power?' And my answer to that question will be: 'It is not possible.'

II

Let me begin with my first question, which bears upon the international, rather than upon the national, meaning of prestige. The word is, as you know, one of those French words which we use in England in a sense different from that in which they are used in France. I admit that in recent years French journalists and political writers have tended to use the word in the English sense rather than in the sense advocated by their own Academicians; and that it would be possible to find even in a reputable French newspaper a phrase such as 'le prestige britannique est fortement engagé', which means very much the same as 'British prestige is seriously involved'. Yet if we are rightly to appreciate the associations possessed by a given word in a foreign language it is desirable to examine the literary rather than the journalistic employment of that word; and in French classical literature the word 'prestige', although not often used, is invariably used with a lively sense of its disreputable origins. Nor is this sense diminished by the chance similarity which prestige bears to their own word for conjurer, *prestidigitateur*. It is not surprising therefore that to the French mind the word 'prestige' should sometimes carry with it associations of fraudulence. At its best, it conveys to them something akin to our own words 'glamour' and 'romance'. At its worst, it suggests the art of the illusionist if not a deliberate desire to deceive. Thus when we speak confidently to our French friends of 'maintaining British prestige' we are apt (as we are so frequently apt) to convey to them a distorted impression of our purposes.

True it is that the word is losing its former values in France even as it is being modified over here. It would be an exaggeration to say that in modern French the word always possesses a disreputable flavour. But it would be correct to say that it carries with it the suggestion, if not of something fraudulent, then certainly of something adventitious. Let me give an illustration. One of the most hackneyed uses of the word occurs in the phrase 'le prestige de son nom'—as it might be journalistically applied to a descendant of Lafayette attending the centenary of the surrender of Yorktown, or to a descendant of the Duke of Wellington unveiling a war memorial at

Quatre Bras. Now in English we should not say on such an occasion 'the great-grandson of Lafayette brings with him the prestige of his name', we should say something like 'the magic glamour of the name of Lafayette'. It is perhaps only a small difference, but I think that it is a real difference. It implies that even in current journalism our own use of the word is more practical, more political and far less sentimental than is the French use.

In Italian the substantive *prestigio*, and even more so the adjective *prestigioso*, is still used to describe something dazzling, deceptive or legendary; and when employing the word to denote the more serious aspects of political reputation, the Italians tend to retain it in its French form rather than to use their own Italian word.

In German the word 'prestige' is regarded as a definitely foreign word and, when used, is used in one of three senses. In the first sense it corresponds to their word *Ansehen* or 'esteem'. In the second sense it is akin to that ridiculous

German word *der Nimbus*, which again is very close to our word 'glamour'. And in the third sense, I fear, it is used as a variant for the phrase 'national honour'. When a German lays it down that any given problem has become a *Prestige-Frage* he is getting very near to describing it as 'a question of National Honour' —a description which, with its implications of hysterical obstinacy, is apt to fill the gentle souls of our own diplomatists with saddened dismay.

I do not propose to weary you any longer with purely dictionary discussions. I have said enough to indicate that few grammarians would contend that an accepted international meaning of the word 'prestige' can in any way be said to exist. What is interesting and important is not these differences of terminology, but the deeper and wider differences which exist in the general concept. An examination of these differences will show, I think, that the English interpretation of prestige is in fact different from that obtaining in other countries; and that our whole conception of both 'reputation' and 'power' is peculiar to ourselves. I shall now pass from the word 'prestige' to the ideas which that word suggests to different nations.

III

I have already suggested that to the French prestige implies an emotion rather than a method. It is not merely that the word itself possesses associations akin to those of our own word 'glamour'; it is also that the general concept belongs for them rather to the category of feelings than to the category of action or of thought. Emotionally the word is not unrelated to such other words as *la gloire* on the one side or *panache* on the other. I am not implying that such words, and the feelings aroused by them, do not have an important effect upon French policy. I am only suggesting that, whereas we regard prestige almost as a political method, the French regard it mainly as an emotional effect.

It may be contended that in making these distinctions I am splitting terminological hairs. It could be argued, for instance, that the French possess a large colonial empire in which they maintain a high level of obedience without the display of overwhelming force. It could be argued again that the French enjoy a reputation among the nations of the world which is perhaps in excess of their actual physical power. And it might be deduced from these arguments that their policy, as ours, must be based upon some political method which we happen to call 'prestige' but which the French happen to call by other names.

I am aware how dangerous it is to generalise regarding the psychology of other countries, but I do not recognise in the processes or methods of French policy any idea which is identical with what we mean in English by the word 'prestige'. The French possess a very definite seventeenth-century sense of domination. They are vividly conscious of the importance of French culture and of its vast exportable value. And they are fully aware that power without reputation is a most uncivilised thing. But the point is that by reputation they mean something different from what we mean. For them, reputation is based partly upon the military capacity of the French race and partly upon their magnificent cultural achievements. For us—with our distrust of purely intellectual values and our irritating passion for confusing the ethical with the practical—reputation is based upon character and conduct. The French tendency, in other words, is to render unto Caesar the things that are God's; whereas our tendency is to render unto God the things that are Caesar's.

How do these differences affect the concept of prestige? In this way, I think. Whereas the French, with their great gifts of precision, are apt to regard power and reputation as two different things—the one belonging to the realm of fact and the other to the realm of feeling—we, with our preference for the imprecise, endeavour to fuse the two into that curious amalgam which we call by the name of 'prestige'.

An even greater difference exists between the British and the German concept of prestige. That tragic lack of self-confidence which is one of the major afflictions of their race inspires Germans with an almost hysterical craving for a national form. 'We are', writes Friedrich Sieburg, 'shifting sand, yet in every grain there inheres a longing to combine with all the rest into solid, durable stone.' This sense of spiritual loneliness—I might almost say of spiritual forsakenness—lies at the very root of the German character and explains many of its more perplexing manifestations. It is this which leads the German to seek comfort in the ordered groups of his fellow-countrymen and explains why for him militarism is not only a political instrument but an end in itself, bringing him relief from his own uncertainties, and providing him with that sense of outline, solidity and purpose for which he craves. It is this spiritual loneliness, again, which explains his self-abandonment to the State; his willingness to surrender to the State his freedom, his conscience and his reasoning powers; and his conception of the State as something superhuman and almost theocratic. It is, again, the tremulous diffidence of the German which leads him to place such confidence in quantitative values, whether in the form of exaggerated erudition or in the form of exaggerated force. And finally it is the German's lack of self-confidence which renders him so sensitive, so suspicious, so impulsive and at times so reckless.

Inevitably, for a race thus constituted, the concept of prestige is something more tense, more personal and far less flexible than it is with us. Even as an individual, the German is more prone to take offence than is the Englishman, being more preoccupied than we are by considerations of status. This exaggerated awareness of status often complicates social relations between Germans and their fellow-countrymen and renders them self-conscious in their dealings with foreigners. Upon the concept of prestige it has the following important bearing.

The German tends, as I have said, to surrender his own individuality to the State, and he often does so with superb self-sacrifice. But by this act of surrender he identifies himself with the State to a degree which is not conceivable in this country, and he comes to regard the State with the same passionate susceptibility, the same nervous sense of status, which prove so inconvenient for him in his personal relationships. In this manner his personal honour becomes fused with his national honour, and the resultant form of patriotism is far more inflammable than that old warm blanket which patriotism is with us. Thus the German concept of prestige is very akin to their concept of national honour, and the latter concept is closely identified with the concept of personal honour, which, in its turn, is much concerned with questions of status. And whereas for the Englishman the idea of prestige is impersonal, fluctuating and elastic; for the

German it is something intensely personal, rigid and tense. I do not think that in our past and present dealings with Germany we have always taken sufficiently generous account of this consideration.

IV

So much for my first question. I hope that I have convinced you that the word 'prestige' has no universal meaning but it is differently interpreted in different countries. I now come to my second question, namely: 'What meaning does the word "prestige" possess for the average Englishman?'

It would be agreed I suppose that in its widest sense the word is used by us to signify, not glamour or glory, not national honour, but national reputation. In a narrower sense it implies the extent to which subject races and foreign countries are prepared to believe in our power without that power having either to be demonstrated or exercised. I would suggest, however, that these two definitions are neither sufficiently comprehensive nor sufficiently precise. Our conception of prestige, for instance, is closely identified with our conception of policy, and it is the latter conception which I must first examine.

Let me return for a moment to the contrast between England and Germany. The German conception of policy is essentially the heroic or warrior conception. German diplomacy, for instance, is conducted by military rather than by civilian methods. There is the whole apparatus of alternative campaigns carefully elaborated in advance; of wide flanking movements and sudden captures of strategical points; of the *Kraftprobe*, the ambush and the night attack; of rapid manœuvre and sudden concentration; of surprises and feints. There is the belief in the importance of initiative and secrecy; the desire to maintain the enemy in a state of anxious uncertainty; the confidence in heavy artillery; and above all the conviction that victory is the only possible alternative to defeat.

The English conception of policy is not in the least military. It is mercantile. We conduct our diplomacy, not as heroic warriors, but as rather timid shopkeepers. Except in rare moments of aberration (the worst of which occurred in 1919) we are not out for spectacular diplomatic victories or sensational trials of strength. What we are after is a profitable deal. And we know from long business experience that no deal is profitable which imposes conditions which are incapable of execution, or leaves our customers devoid of all powers of purchase.

This mercantile conception of policy carries with it an equally mercantile conception of prestige. Thus, for us, the idea of prestige is not so much the exercise of power, as the maintenance of our reputation and credit at such a level as will render the exercise of power unnecessary. To that extent it is closely analogous to the general theory of an old-fashioned banking-house, under which credit precedes, creates and maintains power; but does not necessarily derive from it. It is in this sense that, at the outset of this lecture, I gave the English interpretation of prestige as 'power based on reputation, rather than reputation based on power'. That definition, although to my mind correct, does not go far enough. Since if we are to understand the particular interpretation given to the word 'prestige' in this country, we must examine what is meant by these words 'reputation' and 'power' and what relation they bear to each other.

I shall begin with reputation. It would be agreed, I take it, that our reputation is based partly upon present wealth and power, partly upon past achievements and partly upon national character. The question of power will be dealt with later. As regards past achievements, it is necessary to note that many continental historians—when they consider our long list of defeats, humiliations and blunders—are inclined to attribute our far-flung success, not to any prowess on our part, but either to some fiendish brand of cunning or to some supernatural fantasy of chance. We are ourselves at moments dimly conscious of our own inability to think things out in advance; yet any uneasiness which might be occasioned by the spectacle of our own mental inertia is quickly allayed by some slogan such as 'muddling through' or 'we always lose every battle except the last'. To the foreigner, however, the extreme cerebral indolence of the British people constitutes the great riddle of the ages. Very few foreigners understand us well enough to realise how deep and sincere is our aversion from thought. We rush into projects quite blindly, prefacing our action with some self-righteous generalisation or some indignant denial of what, to clearer heads, is quite obviously and inevitably the very thing that we intend to do. If the project fails, we are accused of treachery. If it succeeds, we are accused of hypocrisy. Only very few people, even in this country, realise that in fact we have not the slightest conception of the direction into which our improvisations are bound to lead us.

Thus, although it would be foolish to contend that our past achievements make no contribution at all to the sum of our prestige, yet it is a remarkable and very fortunate fact that this prestige does not rest upon success alone. Again and again have we committed mistakes, or displayed political cowardice, to an extent which would have shaken to its foundations the reputation of any other country. Again and again have we flung our prestige to the four winds, only to find that other nations immediately collect the fragments and restore it to us almost intact. Again and again have we shown ourselves uncertain, unreliable and timid, and yet we still retain, as never before, the esteem of the vast majority of mankind. What is the explanation of this anomaly? I think that there can be only one explanation, namely that our prestige is founded, not so much upon power or success, as upon our national character.

Most Englishmen, I suppose, if asked what were the special virtues of our national character which have given us this solid reputation, would (after a few agonising moments of embarrassment) answer 'Justice, Efficiency and Idealism'. Now a foreigner would disagree with such an answer. He would contend in the first place that our sense of justice is not necessarily in advance of that possessed by other countries. Our claim to efficiency would bring a pitying but not unfriendly smile to his lips. Whereas at the mention of idealism he would become seriously annoyed. Yet if he were a friendly and intelligent foreigner, and one who had studied our history and explored our strange sub-conscious temperament, he would, I think, answer the same question somewhat as follows.

First among our virtues he would place honesty. He would mean by that, not merely the ordinary every-day honesty of a commercial race, not merely the high standards of our political life, not only a certain general candour, a prevailing habit of truthfulness, but predominantly our constant endeavour to approximate public to private morality. Secondly, he would place what he would probably call 'chivalry', but which I prefer to call 'gentleness'. By that he would mean a constant regard for weaker people, a dislike of bullying, a sympathy with the oppressed, and above all a fine gift of tolerance. Third would come 'objectivity', by which he would mean no more and no less than our unrivalled capacity for seeing the other person's point of view. And he would conclude his list of virtues with the word 'unity', meaning thereby not merely our sense of the organic nature of our country, but the curious fact that in most vital issues the majority of Englishmen are apt—or should I say *were* apt?—to think alike.

This list of amiable virtues does, I think, describe those aspects of the British character which are most esteemed abroad and on which our reputation, and therefore our prestige, is based. It should be noted, however, that there are other countries, and notably Switzerland

and Sweden, which possess these very virtues to an even greater degree and yet whose prestige is not comparable with our own. It might be contended that the reason for this disparity is that the virtues of gentleness, honesty and objectivity shine with a richer lustre when combined with immense wealth and power. But it might also be contended that the reason why Switzerland and Sweden do not possess prestige comparable with that of the British Empire is that prestige is not a question of virtue but of guns. The truth, I think, lies somewhere between these two contentions. The moral reputation of Sweden or Switzerland stands, I should suppose, even higher than our own; yet their prestige is lower than ours, not because they lack guns, but because this deficiency prevents them from rendering their virtues internationally effective. Which consideration brings me to my last question, namely, the problem of power.

V

At the outset of this lecture I suggested that for the average Englishman the meaning of prestige was 'power based on reputation rather than reputation based on power'. In my last section I examined the nature of reputation and concluded that our own reputation was mainly founded upon national character. It remains for me to consider the nature of power, and the proportions in which it must be mixed with reputation if they are both to create prestige.

The cynic at this stage will exclaim: 'But you are raising a false issue. It is obvious, and Hitler and Mussolini have proved it, that prestige is based upon power alone. However high may be your reputation, unless you also possess power you have no prestige. Conversely, however low your reputation may be, so long as you have sufficient power, then prestige follows inevitably. In fact "power" and "prestige" are synonymous terms.'

The answer to that assertion is that 'power' and 'prestige' are *not* synonymous, since, although you cannot *acquire* prestige without power, yet you cannot *retain* prestige without reputation. Moreover, a prestige which contains a high percentage of reputation is able to withstand a loss of power; whereas even a temporary decline in power will destroy a prestige which is devoid of reputation. For instance, at the time of the Abyssinian episode, we exposed to the world a flagrant decline in our power, yet our prestige (much to our surprise) remained almost undamaged; whereas it is inconceivable that any State whose prestige was based on power alone could have survived a similar discomfiture. Again, we maintain our rule over subject peoples, not by the employment of power so much as by the general confidence inspired by reputation. The problem is not, therefore, one of power alone; it is a problem of the proportions in which power and reputation should be mixed.

Power, for our present purposes, may be

regarded as of two kinds, namely, offensive and defensive. Until quite recently the defensive power of Great Britain was immense, and when we are tempted to become self-righteous about our virtues it is as well to remember that it was our invulnerability which allowed those virtues to develop. Our unchallenged security during the course of the nineteenth century enabled us to build up our Empire and to create our prestige with a minimum expenditure of force. Yet to contend that we acquired our Empire merely by the exercise of our more agreeable qualities would be to advance a contention which is untrue. Our fathers, with their long habit of security, were frequently unjust in condemning the militarism of other countries when our own navalism was as excessive as it could be. Nor is it accurate to quote the low figures of our standing army as proof that our Empire and our prestige were both acquired without the use of force. Our potential power was, owing to our unassailability, immeasurable.

But that is not the point. The point is that we exercised that power with very careful regard for our reputation.

Take, for instance, the end of the Napoleonic wars when our prestige and potency were at their height. Although at that time we might have acquired half the world, we were content with a quite modest booty. We abandoned Martinique, Senegal and Gambia to our former enemy; and we gave the East Indian islands to somebody else. Nor were these surrenders dictated by lassitude or repletion. They were deliberately made in order to increase our reputation and thus to cement our prestige with something deeper and more durable than power alone. 'I am sure,' wrote Castlereagh to Lord Liverpool, 'I am sure our reputation on the Continent, as a feature of strength, power and confidence is of more real moment to us than any such acquisitions which might be made.' It is unfortunate that a similar regard for reputation did not guide our counsels in 1919.

Let me take another and more recent instance. On 1 January 1907 Sir Eyre Crowe, at
that time head of the Western Department of
the Foreign Office, wrote a memorandum regarding the foundations of British policy. In
that memorandum he laid it down as an axiom
that we must maintain the mastery of the seas
against any possible enemy. Yet he added an
important corollary. He pointed out that this
maritime supremacy would, if abused, arouse
feelings of resentment and jealousy throughout
the world. Our power, he said, must therefore
be exercised with the utmost benevolence and
with the minimum of provocation. Our policy
must 'be closely identified with the primary
and vital interests of a majority of other
nations'. What were those primary interests?
The first was independence and the second was
trade. Sir Eyre Crowe therefore laid it down
that British policy must maintain free trade
and must at the same time display 'a direct and
positive' interest in the independence of small
nations. Does that wise and generous tradition

still maintain among us? I fear that it has suffered a decline.

I have cited these two instances in order to show that even when in possession of un-challengeable power we were sufficiently sensible to realise that power, without reputation, is not enough. We are now no longer possessed of unchallengeable power. Our defensive power has rapidly, I might almost say suddenly, diminished, whereas the offensive power of other nations has correspondingly increased. We have been able, because of our reputation, to maintain our prestige in spite of the humiliations which we have undergone. Yet it would be folly to suppose that we shall continue to maintain it by the force of reputation alone; and all reasonable people will agree that the proportion of power in our prestige must rapidly and largely be augmented.

We shall not fall, I trust, into the opposite extreme and forget, once we have again achieved great power, that power is not enough. I earnestly hope that, with mounting armaments, we shall be more scrupulous than ever to maintain our reputation. I described that reputation as being based, above all, upon our national character. Is there no danger lest that character may also decline?

For why was it that we, during all those years of supremacy, were gentle, tolerant and kind? Why was it that we, more than any other nation, were able to achieve some approximation between public and private morality? Why was it that we were always ready to defy the powerful and to protect the weak? I have not that complacency which would lead me to believe that our people are possessed of nobler virtues than are other peoples. We could afford the luxury of gentleness because we were completely unafraid. Now that we have lost our sense of security, shall we always maintain our good humour or our objectivity? Will even our honesty, our candour and our truthfulness remain undimmed? And are we sure, even, that our unity is certain to survive the clash of economic religions? If we are alert and determined, these great blessings will each one of them be preserved. Yet if we forfeit them, then (however great may be our physical power, however thunderous our guns) British prestige will perish from the earth; and mankind will thereby lose one of the last citadels of tolerance, of gentleness and of reason.